my Kentucky garden

a gardener's journal

Denny McKeown

Copyright © 2000 Denny McKeown

All rights reserved. No part of this book may be reproduced or transmitted in any form or by any means, electronic or mechanical, including photocopying, recording, or by any information storage or retrieval system, without permission from the publisher.

ISBN 1-930604-09-2

NOTE: The ideas expressed in this book are not, in all cases, exact quotations, as some have been edited to fit the format. In all cases, the publisher has attempted to maintain the speaker's original intent. Further, in some cases, source materials for this book were obtained from secondary sources, primarily print media and the Internet. While every effort has been made to ensure the accuracy of these sources, accuracy cannot be guaranteed. To notify us of any corrections or clarifications, please contact Cool Springs Press.

Cool Springs Press, Inc.
112 Second Avenue North
Franklin, TN 37064

First Printing 2000
Printed in the United States of America
10 9 8 7 6 5 4 3 2 1

Design by:	Sheri Ferguson
Illustrations by:	Allison Starcher
Editorial Consultant:	Erica Glasener

Visit the Cool Springs Press website at www.coolspringspress.com

my Kentucky garden

a gardener's journal

this is my

Kentucky

garden

Beth Leister
name

Spring   2002
year

why keep a garden journal ?

Welcome! We busy Kentucky gardeners are often seeking a high-performance, low-maintenance landscape. But we take pride in our gardens and know that gardening is a constant learning process. That's why you will enjoy *My Kentucky Garden: A Gardener's Journal.*

Keeping a garden journal will help you keep track of how your garden grows. You will discover which plants thrive, which ones struggle, and best of all, you will discover many surprises. More than just record keeping, journaling is a way to trace your growth as a gardener. Writing down your favorite moments in the garden may help you decide which plants to add or which to replace. How does your garden make you feel? You may discover you prefer one season to another. Maybe your style of gardening has changed. A journal will help you track the evolution in your garden.

As gardeners know, weather is a huge factor in plant performance. By keeping track of air temperature, the amount of rainfall, and drastic changes (storms or droughts), we can see which plants survived and plan better for next year.

Has the environment in your garden changed? Trees and shrubs that were once small may have matured and created a shadier garden. Keeping a list of what you plant, where and when you plant it, and the source of the plant will provide useful information for the future.

Further, keeping up with what's blooming when, and how long it blooms is another reason to write daily or weekly in a garden journal. You might be surprised at how many seasons your garden features beautiful blooms, colorful foliage, or fantastic fruits. Some of the best color combinations happen by accident and remembering which plant blooms and when it blooms from year to year is not easy. With good journal records, you may recreate pleasing plant combinations and avoid repeating mistakes.

How often you fertilize, prune, and water are other things to keep track of in your garden journal. Which techniques have been most successful? If you have a particular pest or disease problem with one plant, what methods were effective in eradicating or controlling the problem? If your roses were beautiful last year, when did you prune them and how much did you prune? When did you divide your phlox and where did you plant the different varieties of spring bulbs? All of these questions can be answered in the pages of *My Kentucky Garden*.

getting started with your garden journal

By keeping daily records, you can check your journal and chart your most successful garden practices. Whether it's how and when you planted a favorite hydrangea or rose, when the first iris came into bloom, or when you noticed the scent of a particular viburnum, your Kentucky garden journal will provide the ideal format for keeping in touch with your garden and what it can teach you. Here's how to begin.

- Designate a day and a time during the week to write in your journal. You might discover that early morning coffee time or the end of the day works best.
- Use a favorite pen and keep it with your journal. Write brief, clear notes (*rainy and cool with temp around 60°F, Phlox 'David' has been in bloom for 2 weeks, Butterfly Bush loaded with flower buds, planted two daylilies in perennial garden*).
- Keep a 5"x 7" envelope tucked in the back of your journal to hold photographs and pictures from catalogs or magazines that inspire you. Be sure to identify and label pictures.
- List existing trees, shrubs, perennials, and bulbs, including a sketch of where they are located. This will be especially helpful over the years when you make changes in your garden.

Once you get used to journaling, you may find that you look forward to writing about your garden as much as you enjoy adding new plants.

{ introduction }

Many of us buy plants that strike our eyes, giving no consideration to the location in which we plan to plant them. Canadian hemlock and rhododendron, for example, need special growing conditions to thrive. Roses often wind up in too much shade because we have convinced ourselves that two hours of sun are as good as five.

The USDA cold-hardiness zone map will help you understand your growing environment. A cold-hardiness zone is defined by the northernmost boundary in which plants can grow when the weather is at its coldest. Kentucky primarily has one, zone 6.

Study the environmental conditions in your garden and let the garden tell you what to do. Familiarize yourself with the native or common plants of your region and use them as a guide to selections for your garden, both native and exotic. Knowing the type of soil, light, and exposure your plants require will help you select the right plant for the right place. You will probably want to select plants that tolerate your landscape's climate to increase survival and minimize maintenance. With the exception of large trees and shrubs, don't be afraid to move your plants. The best time to do this is in early spring, before the new growth appears. Often conditions change, and what was once a favorable environment may no longer be. Proper watering, mulch, and fertilizer further help to ensure the success of your garden.

the plan

It can be useful to consult a professional landscape designer or architect to help you plan your garden. Their work can be as detailed as a drawing with every plant sited or as broad as a simple list of recommended plants for particular areas. If you have just moved into your house, observe the garden one whole growing season before you hire someone to help you develop a plan. This experience will help you determine which areas receive the most light and which are in shade, etc. Once you have a plan, you can implement it in stages over time. Making adjustments as conditions or your tastes change is easy.

You may also refer to my book, *Kentucky Gardener's Guide* (Cool Springs Press, 2000), for specific plant recommendations and advice for Kentucky gardeners.

soil

Good soil is essential for a fruitful garden and is the foundation of our landscape. There are parts of Kentucky that have very good soil, while other parts of Kentucky have sandy soil.

Soil is composed of mineral material, organic matter, water, and air. The mineral matter comes from the weathering of bedrock, which combines with organic matter from dead plants, manure, and other decomposing materials. It is important to know what type of soil you have in order to garden successfully.

amending your soil

For years, it was standard practice to tell homeowners installing new plants to amend the soil and to add peat moss, compost, manure, and all the above to the soil you dug out while digging the hole. Common sense is now convincing the industry to tell you that it is possible to overamend your soil. What kind of soil is the plant going to grow in once the roots grow beyond the hole you dug? Overimproving the existing soil, or worse, yet, replacing the old soil with fresh topsoil creates what I call "bathtubbing". When it rains or when we water, the moisture goes through the overamended soil very quickly, hitting the

hard clay bottom and filling up like a
bathtub. Too much water equals
a dead plant.

I recommend using organic peat
or pine bark chips to amend soil
when needed, but do not add more
than 30% amendments to mix with the
existing soil. Always break up your clay soil
so no particle is bigger than a golf ball. Compost is
one of the best soil amendments available because it is alive with billions
of creatures that help roots absorb water and nutrients. Making
compost can be as simple as piling leaves and clippings in a heap and
letting them break down. You can add kitchen waste such as coffee
grounds, clean eggshells, and uncooked vegetable scraps to your
compost pile. It is best not to add animal fats, bones, or meat. Be
patient! It will take approximately six months and a 30-gallon bag of
yard trimmings to yield 1 cubic foot of compost from your pile.

watering

Watering seems like a simple thing, but gardeners have a tendency
to overwater or underwater plants. Sandy soils drain quickly, requiring
watering often during blistering summers. Clay soils hold water,
therefore plants growing in clay need less watering. Don't water by
a schedule. Always check the soil with a garden towel, digging down
4-5 inches, to see if moisture is needed.

guidelines for watering:

- Water your container plants until the water runs out the bottom. During
  hot summer months some containers may need water twice a day. Do
  not water until the top inch of the soil is dry to the touch.
- Put a hose at the base of a newly installed tree or shrub and thoroughly
  soak the rootball when it's dry. As the plant grows, the area that needs
  to be soaked will increase as the root zone increases.

- Use shallow cans (tuna, etc.) to measure the amount of water applied by your lawn sprinkler. Put six cans in the area you are watering and run the system for an hour. Then measure the depth of the water in all cans. When the average depth of the water is 1 inch, the grass root zone has been irrigated. This may take one to four hours.
- Buy an inexpensive water timer and a few soaker hoses. They are a worthwhile investment. During periods of drought mature trees will benefit from long, slow watering.

mulch

Mulch discourages weeds and retains moisture. It acts like a blanket, holding moisture in the soil and keeping the soil temperature from getting too hot or cold.

Mulch can also help reduce weed infestations. But use common sense! Too much mulch can prevent air and water from getting to the plants' roots. Some plants mulch themselves with their own foliage spread.

tips when mulching:

- Apply a 1- to 2-inch layer of mulch on top of the soil around all plants. At the same time, avoid piling mulch against the trunks or stems of plants. This could lead to potential disease problems.
- Hardwood chips, shredded leaves, and compost are good choices.

nutrients

The main nutrients plants need are nitrogen, phosphorous, and potassium. When you buy fertilizer you will see three numbers on the bag representing the percentage by weight of each nutrient in the mixture. For example, a bag of 10-10-10 fertilizer contains 10%

nitrogen (N), 10% phosphorus (P), and 10% potassium (K). The other 70% is inert filler.

Each nutrient serves a function in the overall good health of a plant. Nitrogen promotes leaf growth. That is why lawn fertilizer has a high nitrogen percentage. Phosphorous is important in the formation of roots, as well as flower, seed, and fruit growth. That is why starter fertilizers and bloom fertilizers have high percentages of phosphorous. Potassium increases overall cell health. When plants are under stress from drought or cold, adequate potassium helps them withstand the crisis.

soil test

A soil test helps determine how much fertilizer to apply and whether any additives (such as lime) are needed. The Kentucky Extension Service can provide you with the necessary forms and information for soil testing, or you can contact a state-certified, soil-testing laboratory.   Soil acidity is measured in numbers from 1 to 14 on the pH scale, where 7 is neutral. Most plants prefer a soil that has a pH of 6.0 to 6.5. The soil test report will tell you how much and what type of fertilizer or other additives to use for the type of plant you are growing, and the soil pH and what, if anything, should be done to protect it.

get started journaling and have fun

Your garden is what you make it. If you keep your heart and mind open to the nuances of nature, you will cultivate more than just pretty flowers and strong trees. Both you and your plants will grow in your beautiful garden. Hopefully, you will also have fun creating lovely gardens.
HAPPY GARDENING!

Kentucky Garden Favorites

I selected a list of plants that are easy to grow, readily available, adaptable to various growing conditions, and help provide year-round interest. These plants can be very beneficial to your Kentucky garden because they provide brilliant color, some attract birds and wildlife, and most require minimal maintenance. You will find most of my recommendations in my book, *Kentucky Gardener's Guide* (Cool Springs Press, 2000). Give these a try!

Annuals

- Scaevola — *Scaevola aemula*
- Vinca — *Catharanthus roseus*
- Impatiens — *IImpatiens wallerana*
- Melampodium — *Melampodium paludosum*
- Million Bells® — *Calibrachoa* hybrids
- Petunias — *Petunia* x *hybrida*
- Blue Salvia — *Salvia farinacea*
- Wax-Leaf Begonia — *Begonia* hybrids
- Pentas — *Pentas lanceolata*
- Torenia — *Torenia fournieri*

Perennials

- Daylily — *Homerocallis hybrids*
- Pincushion Flower — *Scabiosa caucasica* 'Fama'
- Hosta — *Hosta* spp. and hybrids
- Black-Eyed Susan — *Rudbeckia fulgida* var. *sullivantii* 'Goldsturm'
- Stokes' Asters — *Stokesia laevis*
- Coreopsis — *Coreopsis verticillata* 'Moonbeam'
- Garden Mum — *Chrysanthemum* x *morifolium*
- Gayfeather — *Liatris spicata*
- Astilbe — *Astilbe* x *arendsii*
- Coneflower — *Echinacea purpurea*

Bulbs

- Daffodil — *Narcissus* species and cultivars
- Caladium — *Caladium* x *hortulanum*
- Allium — *Allium* spp.
- Crocus — *Crocus vernus*
- Dahlia — *Dahlia* hybrids
- Tulips — *Tulipa* cultivars
- Scilla — *Scilla siberica*
- Grape Hyacinth — *Muscari* spp.
- Tuberous Begonia — *Begonia* x *tuberhybrida*
- Canna — *Canna* x *generalis*

Vines

- Clematis — *Clematis* hybrids
- Climbing Hydrangea — *Hydrangea anomala* spp. *petiolaris*
- Virginia Creeper — *Parthenocissus quinquefolia*
- Mandevilla — *Mandevilla* x *amabilis*
- Boston Ivy — *Parthenocissus tricuspidata*
- Trumpet Vine — *Campsis radicians*
- Silver Lace Vine — *Polygonum aubertii*
- Wisteria — *Wisteria floribunda*
- Moonflower — *Ipomoea alba*
- Morning Glory — *Ipomoea purpurea*

Turfgrasses

- Turf-Type Tall Fescue — *Festuca* cultivars
- Kentucky Blue Grass — *Poa* cultivars
- Fine-Leaf Fescue — *Festuca* cultivars
- Perennial Rye — *Lolium* cultivars
- Zoysia — *Zoysia* cultivars

Trees

- Flowering Crabapple — *Malus* spp. and cultivars
- Serviceberry — *Amelanchier arborea*
- Ornamental Pear — *Pyrus calleryana*
- Sweet Bay Magnolia — *Magnolia virginiana*
- Eastern Redbud — *Cercis canadensis*
- Carolina Silver Bell — *Halesia carolina*
- 'Winter King' Hawthorn — *Crataegus virdis* 'Winter King'
- American Holly — *Ilex opaca*
- Kentucky Coffeetree — *gymnocladus dioicus*
- Japanese Tree Lilac — *Syringa reticulata*

Shrubs

- Blue Maid Holly — *Ilex* x *meservaea* 'Blue Maid'
- Goldencup St. Johnswort — *Hypericum patulum* 'Sungold'
- Korean Boxwood — *Buxus microphylla* var. *koreana*
- Dwarf Spirea — *Spiraea* x *bumalda*
- Butterfly Bush — *Buddleia davidii*
- Viburnum 'Alleghany' — *Viburnum* x *rhytidophylloides*
- Bayberry — *Myrica pensylvanica*
- Itea — *Itea virginica*
- Hummingbird Clethra — *Clethra alnifolia* 'Hummingbird'

Ground covers

- English Ivy — *Hedera helix*
- Wintercreeper — *Euonymus fortunei* 'Coloratus'
- Lily Turf — *Liriope muscari*
- Ajuga — *Ajuga reptans*
- Pachysandra — *Pachysandra terminalis*
- Myrtle — *Vinca minor*
- Creeping Juniper — *Juniperus* cultivars
- Lily-of-the-Valley — *Convallaria majalis*
- Chameleon Plant — *Houttuynia cordata*
- Creeping Phlox — *Phlox subulata*

Ornamental grasses

- Fountain Grass — *Pennisetum alopecuroides* 'Hameln'
- Maiden Grass — *Miscanthus sinensis* 'Gracillimus'
- Japanese Blood Grass — *Imperata cylindrical* 'Rubra'
- Feather Reed Grass — *Calamagrostis* x *acutiflora* 'Overdam'
- Blue Fescue — *Festuca ovina* 'Glauca'
- Northern Sea Oats — *Chasmanthium latifolium*
- Ribbon Grass — *Phalaris arundinacea* 'Picta'
- Ravenna Grass (Northern Pampas Grass) — *Erianthus*

Roses

- Hedge Rose — *Rosa* 'Bonica' Meidiland™
- Shrub Rose — *Rosa* 'Carefree Beauty'
- Climbing Rose — *Rosa* 'Golden Showers'
- Miniature Rose — *Rosa* 'Lady Sunblaze'
- Grandiflora Rose — *Rosa* 'Fame'
- Hybrid Tea Rose — *Rosa* 'Show Biz'

kentucky garden favorites

{ kentucky hardiness zone map }

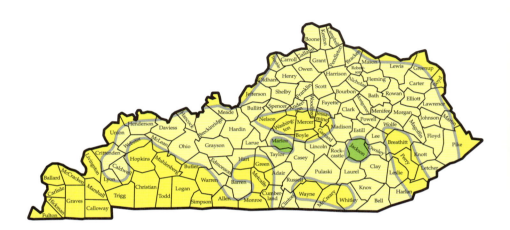

Average Annual Minimum Temperature

5A	-15° F to -20° F
5B	-10° F to -15° F
6A	-5° F to -10° F
6B	0° F to -5° F

*To create a
little flower is the
labour of ages.*

— *William Blake*

january | week 1

January

garden observations

what's the weather like?

Start the year off right! Photograph your garden at least once every month. This will help you with your planning and planting schemes.

what have I planted/transplanted?

garden notes

What is a weed? A plant whose virtues have not yet been dicovered.
—Ralph Waldo Emerson

tending my garden

january | week 1

january | week 2

January

garden observations

Order seeds now for your favorite annuals, perennials and vegetables. Cut out color photographs and create your own record for what you order.

what's the weather like?

When planning your garden, use a large sheet of graph paper with 1/4 inch grids. A scale of 1 inch = 4 feet is a useful proportion.

what have I planted/transplanted?

garden notes

tending my garden

january | week 2

january | week 3

January

garden observations

what's the weather like?

what have I planted/transplanted?

garden notes

> Check house plants for signs of insects and disease. Spots, speckles or webs on leaves indicate pests are present.

tending my garden

january | week 3

january | week 4

January

garden observations

what's the weather like?

Tip to Remember:
You may also use
vegetables as
ornamental plants.
Ornamental peppers
and sweet potato vine
selections are good
examples.

what have I planted/transplanted?

garden notes

tending my garden

january | week 4

february | week 1

February

garden observations

what's the weather like?

Take a walk through your garden, and plan additions to create winter interest for next year.

what have I planted/transplanted?

Did You Know? The only tulip color that has not yet been developed is any shade of blue.

garden notes

tending my garden

february | week 1

february | week 2

February

garden observations

what's the weather like?

When in doubt, call your local Extension Service. Master Gardeners there will provide information (and the advice is free!)

what have I planted/transplanted?

garden notes

tending my garden

february | week 2

february | week 3

garden observations

daffodils are starting to bloom

Extend the life of your cut flowers. Remove the lower leaves and re-cut the stems before arranging them in lukewarm water.

what's the weather like?

Sunny - partly Cloudy @ 45 degrees.

what have I planted/transplanted?

garden notes

I haven't planted
or transplanted yet.
Looking forward to.
it (maybe this coming
weekend.

tending my garden

february | week 3

Though I do not believe
that a plant will spring
up where no seed has been,
I have great faith in a
seed. Convince me that
you have a seed there,
and I am prepared to
expect wonders.

— Henry David Thoreau

february | week 4

February

garden observations

what's the weather like?

Tip to Remember:
Fill clear plastic
milk jugs with
water and place
around young
tomato plants.
They will provide
warmth overnight
for young plants,
helping you get a
jump on spring.

what have I planted/transplanted?

garden notes

tending my garden

february | week 4

march | week 1
March

what's blooming?

Direct sow wildflower seeds where you want them to grow in climates with USDA zones 1 through 6. (Check the zone map in the introduction to identify your zone.)

what's the weather like?

Take a soil test now so you will know how to prepare your garden for the next season.

what have I planted/transplanted?

garden notes

tending my garden

march | week 1

march week 2

March

what's blooming?

Tip to Remember:
Plan to add a few
annuals to your
perennial garden
to help provide
season-long blooms.

what's the weather like?

Watch for aphids on
shrubs as they leaf out.
Treat with insecticidal
soap or any other
labeled pesticide,
if needed.

what have I planted/transplanted?

Start tomato seeds for
transplants 4-6 weeks
before optimum plant-
ing time in your area.

garden notes

tending my garden

march | week 2

march | week 3

what's blooming?

Single-flower forms of marigolds and zinnias are more appealing to butterflies than the double-flower forms.

what's the weather like?

Did You Know? Viburnum is a member of the honeysuckle family.

what have I planted/transplanted?

garden notes

tending my garden

march | week 3

march | week 4

March

what's blooming?

what's the weather like?

Hummingbirds love tubular flowers such as trumpet vine, coral honeysuckle, and nicotiana. Plant lots of these if you want to attract hummingbirds.

what have I planted/transplanted?

garden notes

tending my garden

march | week 4

Half the interest of a garden is the constant exercise of the imagination.

— C.W. Earle

april | week 1

what's blooming?

April 7th - my B-day
Creeping Phlox is Blooming
Bleeding hearts &
Azaleas. azaleas don't look
very good.

what's the weather like?

It's around 60° & 70°

Have you photographed your garden lately? This will help with your garden planning and design ideas.

An easy time to weed is the day after a gentle rain, when the soil is slightly moist, and weeds are easy to pull—roots and all.

what have I planted/transplanted?

In the front - concrete pots. I planted 12 ferns in the shade and pansey's everywhere else

garden notes

(This week)
I also plan to plant cabbage in the back yard and a tomatoe plant in a pot on the deck. With the dogs, who knows what will happen.

tending my garden

april | week 1

april | week 2

April

Propagate some of your favorite broadleaf shrubs using this simple layering technique: Select a branch that is close to the ground. Bend the branch so that it is in contact with the soil. Cover the branch with soil. Water well and hold the branch in place with a brick. In six weeks, check to see if there are roots. Once the roots are firmly established, cut the new plant off from the mother plant.

what's blooming?

Phlox, Crabapple trees, azaleas & our Jane Magnolia

what's the weather like?

80°+ Sunny
Rained 2 days

what have I planted/transplanted?

Cabbage, & seeds of herbs
Pattio tomatoe plant.

garden notes

tending my garden

april | week 2

As is the gardener, such is the garden.

— Hebrew Proverb

april | week 3

April

what's blooming?

Tip to Remember:
When digging a hole
for a tree, it's best to
dig the hole at least
half again as wide as
the size of the rootball
(much wider is even
better). Use the same
soil you dug out to
backfill around
the rootball and
water-in well.

what's the weather like?

80° + Sunny

Turn your compost
pile. If you haven't
started one already,
call your Extension
Service for advice.

what have I planted/transplanted?

Salvia
Coneflower
Black eyed Susans
Coriospis

garden notes

tending my garden

april | week 3

april | week 4

April

what's blooming?

what's the weather like?

Wooden clothespins can be used as plant markers.

Place grow-thru stakes above plants that need support in early spring, and in a short time they will cover the stakes.

what have I planted/transplanted?

garden notes

tending my garden

april | week 4

may week 1
May

Plan to prune back spring-blooming azaleas and other shrubs such as forsythia or spirea after they finish flowering. This way you won't cut off any potential flower buds for next year.

Check plants once or twice a week for insect and disease problems. It's easier to control a small infestation if it's discovered early.

what's blooming?

what's the weather like?

what have I planted/transplanted?

garden notes

tending my garden

may | week 1

may week 2

May

what's blooming?

what's the weather like?

Incorporate a slow-release fertilizer in the soil of hanging baskets and container plantings. This will provide nutrients for several months in one application.

what have I planted/transplanted?

garden notes

Many diseases can be controlled with sanitation. Remove and destroy any infected leaves as soon as they are found.

tending my garden

may | week 2

may week 3

what's blooming?

Parsley and fennel provide food for butterfly caterpillars.

what's the weather like?

Interest children in gardening by planning a small child's garden. A bean tee-pee is fun to plant and grow!

what have I planted/transplanted?

garden notes

> The best time for slug hunting is at night using a flashlight and a pair of gloves.

tending my garden

may | week 3

may week 4

May

what's blooming?

Did You Know?
Bees are our most
efficient pollinators
for flowers, fruits,
and vegetables. Any
garden with lots of
bees is a healthy
environment.

what's the weather like?

what have I planted/transplanted?

garden notes

tending my garden

*Tickle it with a hoe
and it will laugh
into a harvest.*

—English Proverb

may | week 4

june week 1

June

A perennial garden looks wonderful when planted against a background of a wall, a hedge, or evergreen shrubs.

A plant's scientific name consists of a genus and an epithet. The genus and the epithet are always italicized and the genus begins with a capital letter. A third word in the name may refer to a specific variety, called a cultivar. It is set off by single quotation marks.

what's blooming?

what's the weather like?

what have I planted/transplanted?

garden notes

tending my garden

june | week 1

june | week 2

what's blooming?

Use vines to create vertical interest in the garden. If you don't have a wall or fence on which to train them, a lattice or arbor will work.

what's the weather like?

You can create your own portable seep irrigation system by punching a few holes in plastic containers and placing them beside plants that need additional moisture.

what have I planted/transplanted?

garden notes

tending my garden

Though an old man, I am but a young gardener...

— Thomas Jefferson

june | week 2

june | week 3

June

Plan to shear fall-blooming asters to make them bushier and more compact.

what's blooming?

what's the weather like?

Did You Know?
Even though a plant may be identified as self-cleaning, flowers are better off if you deadhead, or remove the spent blooms as often as you can. This will allow the plant to use its energy to make more flowers and leaves instead of making seeds.

what have I planted/transplanted?

garden notes

tending my garden

june | week 3

june week 4

June

what's blooming?

what's the weather like?

BTK (*Bacillus thuringiensis kurstaki*) is an organic biological control that is effective against many caterpillars and is safe to use on vegetable crops. *Bacillus thuringiensis* 'San Diego' is effective against some leafeating beetles.

what have I planted/transplanted?

garden notes

tending my garden

june | week 4

july week 1

Harvest herbs for drying as soon as they come into flower. Bundle them up with a rubber band and hang them on a line in a dark, dry place with good air circulation. To preserve the best flavor once they are dry, store the herbs in airtight containers away from heat and light.

Press some flowers and add to this journal. It's a pretty record of what you planted.

what's blooming?

what's the weather like?

what have I planted/transplanted?

garden notes

tending my garden

july | week 1

july week 2

July

what's blooming?

what's the weather like?

what have I planted/transplanted?

Deadhead hybrid tea roses throughout the summer to encourage more blooms.

garden notes

tending my garden

july | week 2

july week 3

what's blooming?

what's the weather like?

Most unwanted summer heat comes through east- and west-facing windows, not through well-insulated roofs and walls. Plant a deciduous tree for shade.

what have I planted/transplanted?

garden notes

tending my garden

july | week 3

july | week 4

what's blooming?
_____
_____
_____
_____
_____
_____

Plants use calcium to build strong cell walls and stems. Deficiencies can cause blossom-end rot on tomatoes.

what's the weather like?
_____
_____
_____
_____
_____
_____

Did You Know? The Greeks and Romans used lavender in bath water. In fact, the Latin name "lavare" means, "wash".

what have I planted/transplanted?
_____
_____
_____
_____

Tip to Remember: When planting seeds, position them in geometric patterns so that you will be able to distinguish them more easily from weed seedlings.

garden notes

tending my garden

july | week 4

Gardening is the purest of human pleasures.

— Francis Bacon

august | week 1

what's blooming?

what's the weather like?

Preserve basil leaves by mixing them in the blender with a small amount of water. Fill ice cube trays with the mixture. Once they freeze, put them in freezer bags. This way you will have basil to use in your favorite Italian dishes all winter long.

what have I planted/transplanted?

garden notes

tending my garden

august | week 1

august | week 2

August

what's blooming?

For the best selection, order your spring-flowering bulbs or purchase them locally when they become available in your area. Keep them cool and dry until you plant them.

what's the weather like?

Take some photographs of your garden to refer to later when planning for next year.

what have I planted/transplanted?

garden notes

tending my garden

august | week 2

august | week 3

If you haven't already done so, draw a plan of your property showing existing trees and shrubs in relation to your house. Make notes throughout the year indicating those areas that receive full sun, shade or a mix of sun and shade. This will help you to choose the right plant for the right place.

what's blooming?

what's the weather like?

what have I planted/transplanted?

garden notes

tending my garden

august | week 3

august week 4

August

what's blooming?

Water your compost pile when the weather has been dry.

what's the weather like?

Order three or four types of paperwhite narcissus to force at two-week intervals. You will have flowers from Halloween into the New Year!

what have I planted/transplanted?

Continue to harvest vegetables as soon as they are ripe. Regular harvesting increases production.

tending my garden

garden notes

He who plants a garden plants happiness.
—Chinese Proverb

august | week 4

september | week 1

what's blooming?

what's the weather like?

Expand your plant collection by exchanging seeds and plants with fellow gardeners.

what have I planted/transplanted?

Add some shrubs to your garden that will offer winter interest such as colorful bark, or unusual shapes.

garden notes

tending my garden

september | week 1

september | week 2

If you haven't started one already, begin a compost pile and let it overwinter. In six months you should have "black gold" to mix into your garden.

what's blooming?

what's the weather like?

what have I planted/transplanted?

garden notes

The frost hurts not weeds.

—Thomas Fuller

tending my garden

september | week 2

september | week 3

september

what's blooming?

what's the weather like?

what have I planted/transplanted?

garden notes

If your annuals are beginning to look ragged, pull them and replace with some mums, pansies, or flowering kale.

tending my garden

september | week 3

september | week 4

Use dried seed
heads such as sedum
and lotus for fall
decorations.

Visit your favorite
nursery to select a tree
or shrub for that spot
in the garden that
needs something new.

what's blooming?

what's the weather like?

what have I planted/transplanted?

garden notes

tending my garden

september | week 4

october | week 1

what's blooming?

what's the weather like?

Plant a tree in honor of a birth or in memory of a loved one.

Fall leaf color is triggered by cooler temperatures, shorter days, and less light.

what have I planted/transplanted?

garden notes

tending my garden

october | week 1

october | week 2

October

what's blooming?

what's the weather like?

what have I planted/transplanted?

garden notes

Sprinkle annual rye grass seed on top of the soil of pots you are forcing. By the time the bulbs bloom, it will create a green carpet underneath them.

tending my garden

october | week 2

october | week 3

what's blooming?

what's the weather like?

Tip to Remember: Parsley is a good plant for bed edges. It also looks great grown in containers with pansies.

what have I planted/transplanted?

Use golf tees to mark areas where bulbs are planted.

garden notes

Heaven is under our feet as well as over our heads.
— Henry David Thoreau

tending my garden

october | week 3

october | week 4

October

what's blooming?

what's the weather like?

> **Did You Know?** The word 'wort', as in St. John's Wort, is an old English term that means "medicinal plant".

what have I planted/transplanted?

garden notes

tending my garden

october | week 4

november | week 1

November

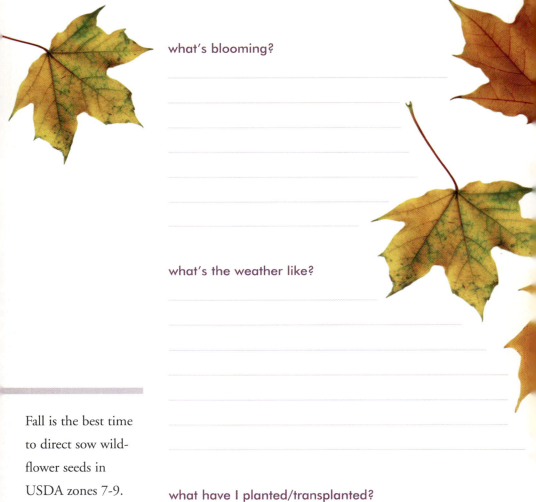

what's blooming?

what's the weather like?

Fall is the best time to direct sow wildflower seeds in USDA zones 7-9. (Check the map in the introduction to verify your zone.)

what have I planted/transplanted?

garden notes

Autumn is a second spring when every leaf is a flower. —Albert Camus

tending my garden

november | week 1

november | week 2

what's blooming?
_____
_____
_____
_____
_____
_____

what's the weather like?
_____
_____
_____
_____
_____
_____

Continue to mow your lawn for as long as it keeps growing.

Clean and sharpen garden tools. Lightly coat with oil to prevent rust.

what have I planted/transplanted?
_____
_____
_____
_____
_____
_____

garden notes

tending my garden

november | week 2

november | week 3

November

what's blooming?

what's the weather like?

what have I planted/transplanted?

garden notes

Extend the life of
your fresh-cut holiday
tree by storing it in a
cool shady place until
you move it indoors.
Re-cut the trunk
before moving it
indoors and use
plenty of fresh water
in the reservoir.

tending my garden

november | week 3

november | week 4

For best results, store unused seeds in a cool, dark place in an air- and water-resistant container.

Selecting the right tool for the job can prevent most injuries. Wear safety gear when operating power equipment.

what's blooming?

what's the weather like?

what have I planted/transplanted?

garden notes

tending my garden

november | week 4

december | week 1

Make a wreath for the holidays. Rose hips, bittersweet, and euonymus are good choices for materials.

garden observations

what's the weather like?

what have I planted/ transplanted?

garden notes

*A garden is a friend
you can visit any time.*
—unknown

tending my garden

december | week 1

december | week 2

December

garden observations

Cast iron plant, Chinese evergreen, heartleaf philodendron, and snake plant will tolerate low-light conditions.

what's the weather like?

Tip to Remember: The winter sun provides the most solar heat through south-facing windows. Avoid planting shade trees or evergreens that may shade these heat-absorbing windows if you need the extra warmth.

what have I planted/transplanted?

garden notes

tending my garden

december | week 2

december | week 3

December

Recycle your holiday tree. The branches can be removed and used as mulch. Or you can leave the tree intact and use it as a windbreak and shelter for birds.

Don't put wood ashes in your compost pile; they will alter the pH level too much.

garden observations

what's the weather like?

what have I planted/transplanted?

garden notes

tending my garden

december | week 3

december | week 4

garden observations

what's the weather like?

what have I planted/transplanted?

garden notes

> Pruning large trees, especially those located near utilities should be performed by a professional. Call a certified arborist if you need trees pruned.

tending my garden

december | week 4

plant inventory/history

name

when planted

where planted

size

source

price

name

when planted

where planted

size

source

price

name

when planted

where planted

size

source

price

name

when planted

where planted

size

source

price

name

when planted

where planted

size

source

price

name

when planted

where planted

size

source

price

name

when planted

where planted

size

source

price

name

when planted

where planted

size

source

price

plant inventory/history

name

when planted

where planted

size

source

price

name

when planted

where planted

size

source

price

name

when planted

where planted

size

source

price

name

when planted

where planted

size

source

price

name

when planted

where planted

size

source

price

name

when planted

where planted

size

source

price

name

when planted

where planted

size

source

price

name

when planted

where planted

size

source

price

plant inventory/history

name	name
when planted	when planted
where planted	where planted
size	size
source	source
price	price

name	name
when planted	when planted
where planted	where planted
size	size
source	source
price	price

name	name
when planted	when planted
where planted	where planted
size	size
source	source
price	price

name	name
when planted	when planted
where planted	where planted
size	size
source	source
price	price

plant inventory/history

name	**name**
when planted	when planted
where planted	where planted
size	size
source	source
price	price
name	**name**
when planted	when planted
where planted	where planted
size	size
source	source
price	price
name	**name**
when planted	when planted
where planted	where planted
size	size
source	source
price	price
name	**name**
when planted	when planted
where planted	where planted
size	size
source	source
price	price

plant inventory/history

name

when planted

where planted

size

source

price

name

when planted

where planted

size

source

price

name

when planted

where planted

size

source

price

name

when planted

where planted

size

source

price

name

when planted

where planted

size

source

price

name

when planted

where planted

size

source

price

name

when planted

where planted

size

source

price

name

when planted

where planted

size

source

price

plant inventory/history

name

when planted

where planted

size

source

price

name

when planted

where planted

size

source

price

name

when planted

where planted

size

source

price

name

when planted

where planted

size

source

price

name

when planted

where planted

size

source

price

name

when planted

where planted

size

source

price

name

when planted

where planted

size

source

price

name

when planted

where planted

size

source

price

plant inventory/history

name		name
when planted		when planted
where planted		where planted
size		size
source		source
price		price

name		name
when planted		when planted
where planted		where planted
size		size
source		source
price		price

name		name
when planted		when planted
where planted		where planted
size		size
source		source
price		price

name		name
when planted		when planted
where planted		where planted
size		size
source		source
price		price

plant inventory/history

name

when planted

where planted

size

source

price

name

when planted

where planted

size

source

price

name

when planted

where planted

size

source

price

name

when planted

where planted

size

source

price

name

when planted

where planted

size

source

price

name

when planted

where planted

size

source

price

name

when planted

where planted

size

source

price

name

when planted

where planted

size

source

price

my garden plan

my garden plan

suppliers & resources

suppliers and resources

photos

photos